Developing Healthy Self-Esteem in Adolescents

by Mary Karsten

Good Apple

A Division of Frank Schaffer Publications, Inc.

Dedication

This book is dedicated to Adelaide Corcoran—a beautiful woman of sparkling intelligence and love. She was my role model.

Executive Editor: Carolea Williams
Editor: Ema Arcellana
Cover and Inside Design: Good Neighbor Press, Inc., Grand Junction, CO
Cover Photograph: Comstock Photography

Entire contents copyright © 1995 by Good Apple, 23740 Hawthorne Boulevard, Torrance, CA 90505-5927. However, the individual purchaser may reproduce designated materials in this book for classroom and individual use, but the purchase of this book does not entitle reproduction of any part for an entire school, district, or system. Such use is strictly prohibited.

ISBN 0-86653-831-3
Printed in the United States of America
1.9 8 7 6 5

Acknowledgments

I would like to thank the many people who have helped in the development and production of this project:

- Joanna Long, my lifelong colleague and personal friend, who always had time for brainstorming and problem solving.
- Rae Haynes and Jean Wilson for their work in the initial presentation of these activities and their support and suggestions in editing.
- All of the EBD students with whom I have worked for the past 11 years and who inspired me to pursue this work.
- The Class of 1989-1990 who participated so enthusiastically in the activities and enjoyed finding my initial spelling errors.
- The International Exchange League which provided me with the opportunity to gain valuable insights from the many fine experts in Behavior Management of the Southern Area of South Australia.
- Des Hurst, Chris Hercock, Jacqui von der Borch, and Maddie Laxton of the Hub Learning Center in Aberfoyle Park, South Australia, for their enthusiastic support and insights.
- The HLC staff for the extensive use of the Center's Macintosh Classic.
- The Southern Area Support Team in Christies Beach, South Australia for their flexibility and support. They also provided me with the opportunities to attend a number of trainings and workshops which inspired me to continue with this project.
- Greg Gause who continually inspired me to complete this project.
- Mary Ellen Zakoff for her consistent belief in my abilities.
- Mary Vesey for providing me with a life foundation which led me into this work and provided me with the inner strength to persist.
- A special thanks to John Bundy, my husband for his consistent and unbelievable patience, tolerance, unlimited cups of coffee and splendid backrubs.

Contents

Introduction 6

Before You Begin 7

Getting to Know Me

Me . . . About Myself 9

Advertising Me 11

Self Silhouette 14

My Name 16

Wrap It Up 20

Assets and Limitations 22

Positive Thinking 25

All About Me 27

Controlling Emotions

Laughing, Laughing, Laughing 32

I Am the Color 35

Dealing with Anger 38

Making Wise Choices

Should I Tell the Truth? 42

Is It Real? 45

Decision-Making Skills 48

The Art of Refusing 52

It's All About Change 56

Taking Responsibility

Are You Prepared? 59

I Was Involved 62

"Cop Outs" 65

Accept Responsibility 69

Improving Communication

How Others See Me 72

Cooperative Effort 75

Communication Clues 77

Listen to Me 82

Setting Goals

Inside of Me 85

How Do I Feel About Myself? 88

I Can Do It 91

The Person I Admire 94

My Dream 96

Evaluation and Review

Me . . . About Myself Re-Evaluation 98

Vocabulary/Concept Review 99

Behavioral Management 102

Journal Starters 105

Visualizations 107

References 112

Introduction

A successful affective education program should address the complex emotional and behavioral needs of today's adolescents. Teaching our youth adaptive prosocial skills gives them the tools to participate more effectively in society. By creating a non-threatening forum where individuals can learn techniques to deal with diverse and often confusing issues, we can help improve the social climate of the community.

As a result of my teaching experience with adolescents, I have realized that many educators are not adequately trained to deal with an adolescent's unique set of problems and behavior. Classroom management programs based mainly on clearly-defined rules and consequences are not enough. Few resources are available for group work dealing with non-therapeutic skills training in the social area. This resource was developed as a result of over two years of research, materials reviews, experience, necessity, and my desire to improve adolescents' self-concept and self-esteem.

This resource is designed to enhance the adolescent's self-concept and self-esteem through decision-making, conflict resolution, and cooperative learning skills and enable students to participate more effectively in society. I hope the easy-to-use activities will benefit all professionals who are concerned about the affective needs of today's adolescents.

Before You Begin

The lessons may be used consecutively or intermittently as issues develop within a group. Choose the method that best meets the needs of your students. Each complete lesson includes journal starters, visualization exercises, the core activity, and a student evaluation. It is important that you include each component of the complete lesson for your students to receive the maximum benefit.

Journal Starters ▶ Writing can be an excellent way for students to express their thoughts and feelings freely. Provide a journal for each student and encourage students to write in it freely and as often as they choose. Each lesson provides sentence starters to inspire students to write about their own thoughts, beliefs, and experiences that relate to the lesson topic. It is suggested that you give students a minimum of 5 minutes of journal-writing time for each lesson. Journal entries may be kept private or shared with the whole group. Additional journal starters are provided on pages 105-106.

Visualizations ▶ Relaxation and mental imagery are important prerequisites for each lesson activity. Visualizations, described for each lesson, should be preceded by a relaxation exercise, such as one of the following.

- Take a deep, slow breath and hold it for a count of four. Slowly release and relax your body and mind as you exhale. (Repeat 3 times.)
- Sit comfortably on the floor with your legs stretched out in front of you. Raise your legs off the floor, tightening the muscles and holding for a count of four. Slowly relax and lower your legs. (Repeat 3 times.)
- Sit up straight with your arms extended out in front of you. Tighten your arms for a count of four. Relax and slowly lower your arms. (Repeat 3 times.)
- Sit up straight while tightening your neck for a count of four. Slowly relax your neck muscles and allow your head to fall. (Repeat 3 times.)

After students are physically relaxed, they can clear their minds through mental imagery—visualizations. Additional visualizations are provided on pages 107-111.

Before You Begin

Activities ▶ Activities give students opportunities to learn about themselves, improve their self-concept, and develop positive interactions with others. Many activities include role plays designed to help students relate to specific situations, dilemmas, and problems. While scenarios are described for each role play, encourage students to create their own dramatizations as well. Invite groups to share life situations and prepare scripts that lead up to the greatest point of conflict. As students perform their dramatizations, have them stop the action at the point of greatest conflict. Encourage audience members to ask questions of the characters and then brainstorm possible solutions.

Each activity ends with an evaluation sheet for students to complete as they reflect on the issues presented in the lesson and how those issues relate to their own lives.

Me... About Myself

Objective: Students will openly and honestly evaluate themselves for the purpose of determining areas they would like to change.

Materials ▶
- overhead projector
- self-evaluation questionnaire on page 10

Introductory Activity ▶

This activity is an effective way to begin the program outlined in this resource. It provides students with an opportunity to honestly assess who they are and take a look at what they might like to change about themselves. This activity may be repeated at the end of the program (see page 98) as an evaluative tool to measure students' progress towards developing healthy self-esteem.

1. Create a transparency of the self-evaluation questionnaire on page 10.
2. Evaluate yourself while inviting group members to listen as you think aloud and verbalize thoughts. Modeling the self-evaluation will encourage students to openly and honestly evaluate themselves.
3. Give each student a self-evaluation questionnaire. Encourage students to honestly evaluate themselves as you guide them through each question.
4. Ask students to share some of their thoughts aloud as they complete the questionnaire.
5. Use group discussion to examine the self-talk of the group leader and the participants.
6. Discuss with students how they can use self-talk as a technique to solve problems. Invite students to describe how they felt as they verbalized their feelings and evaluated their strengths and weaknesses.
7. Keep students' questionnaires if you plan on having students repeat this activity at the end of the program.

Name _____ Date _____

Self-Evaluation

Questionnaire

▶ Evaluate yourself by placing a check mark under the column "Always," "Sometimes," or "Never" for each statement. Be honest and answer as accurately as possible.

		Always	Sometimes	Never
1.	I take good care of myself.	____	____	____
2.	I smile and laugh a lot.	____	____	____
3.	I like to try new things, go new places, and meet new people.	____	____	____
4.	I tell the truth.	____	____	____
5.	I say good things about myself.	____	____	____
6.	Other people see the real me.	____	____	____
7.	I know that I can do many things well.	____	____	____
8.	I feel okay even when I know I can't do something well.	____	____	____
9.	I admit my mistakes.	____	____	____
10.	I know how to handle anger.	____	____	____
11.	I act my age.	____	____	____
12.	I choose not to use illegal drugs.	____	____	____
13.	I choose not to use alcohol.	____	____	____
14.	I know what I need to be healthy emotionally and mentally.	____	____	____
15.	I express my needs to others in positive ways.	____	____	____
16.	I can share my feelings with others.	____	____	____
17.	I stand up for what I believe.	____	____	____
18.	I say good things to others.	____	____	____
19.	I accept compliments.	____	____	____
20.	I accept criticism without feeling bad.	____	____	____
21.	I take risks.	____	____	____
22.	I know when something may be dangerous for me.	____	____	____
23.	I know how to ask for help.	____	____	____
24.	I know how to handle fear.	____	____	____

Advertising Me

Objective: Students will identify their attributes and illustrate them positively and creatively in an advertisement.

Materials ▶
- advertisements, catchy slogans, eye-catching pictures
- colored markers or pencils
- art paper
- magazines
- glue
- scissors
- evaluation on page 13

Journal Starters ▶

The best advertisement I ever saw was . . .
I liked it because . . .
An advertisement catches my eye if it . . .

Visualization ▶

Encourage students to imagine the jobs of their dreams. Tell them the only way to apply for these jobs is to put an advertisement in a magazine. Invite students to visualize an ad that would display their skills and strengths. Remind students that if the ad does not present their best attributes, they may not be hired for their dream jobs.

Activity ▶

1. Display a collection of eye-catching magazine advertisements. Discuss the ads and invite students to verbalize why each ad is appealing. Discuss the elements of an advertisement, such as print styles, colors, and pictures.

2. As a class, brainstorm a list of positive attributes that might be included in an ad written to advertise the qualities of a person.

3. Divide students into pairs. Encourage each student to make a list of attributes that describes him or herself. Invite pairs to work together and share their attributes and feedback with their partners. This sharing is valuable because many times students do not see the good things in themselves that others see.

Advertising Me

4. Distribute materials for students to create advertisements. Students can cut out pictures, words, or phrases from magazines to use in their ads.
5. Display the advertisements in your classroom.
6. Invite each student to complete the evaluation on page 13.

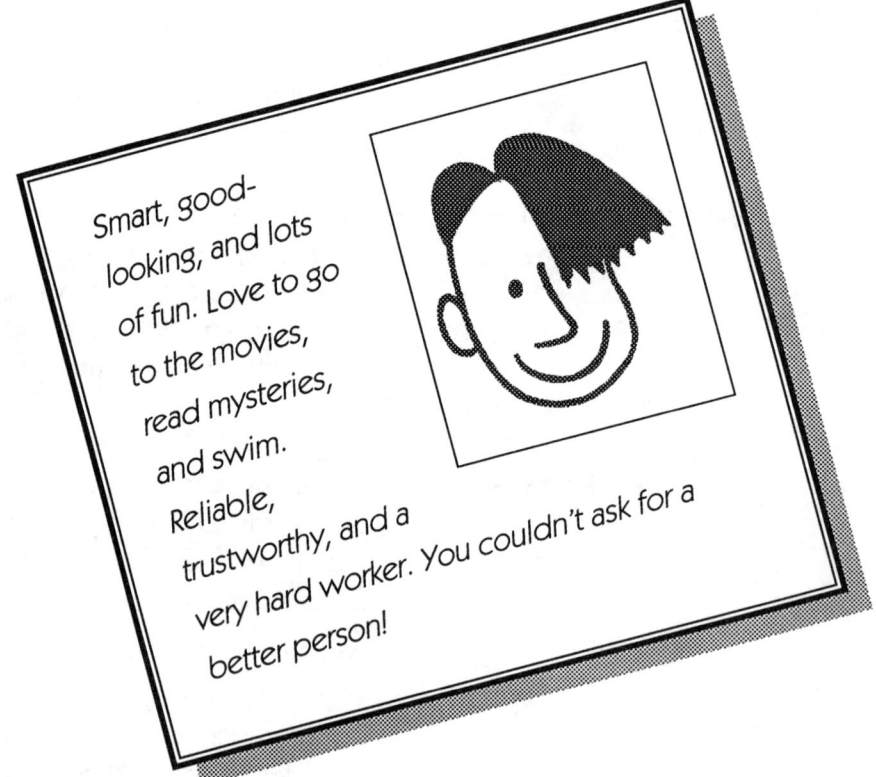

Name _____   Date _____

Advertising Me

Evaluation

▶ Advertising myself is fun because _____
_____
_____
_____
_____

▶ Advertising myself is difficult because _____
_____
_____
_____
_____
_____

▶ I learned some things about myself that I did not know before including _____
_____
_____
_____
_____
_____

▶ The attribute I like best about myself is _____ because
_____
_____
_____
_____

Getting to Know Me - 13

Self Silhouette

Objective: Students will identify personal likes, dislikes, talents, interests, challenges, and attributes and create a collage that represents who they are.

Materials ▶
- overhead projector
- black construction paper
- large pieces of construction paper in various colors
- tape, markers, glue, scissors
- magazines
- evaluation on page 15

Journal Starters ▶
I can show people what I like and who I am by . . .
I am important and I need to let people know that by . . .

Visualization ▶
Invite students to visualize a time and place when they are able to tell their family or friends who they are and how they feel. Encourage students to take their time and think about their likes, dislikes, talents, interests, challenges, and attributes.

Activity ▶

1. Tape black construction paper to the wall. Place an overhead projector facing the wall, so the light shines on the black paper.
2. Divide the class into pairs to trace each other's silhouette on black construction paper using the light shining on the wall.
3. Invite students to cut out their silhouettes and glue them onto colored paper.
4. Have students glue phrases or pictures from magazines to the silhouette that depict their likes, dislikes, talents, interests, challenges, and attributes.
5. After students have created their collages, invite them to share and explain their creations. This is a good opportunity to have a discussion about self-concept and self-esteem.
6. Invite each student to complete the evaluation on page 15.

Name _____   Date _____

Self Silhouette

Evaluation

▶ What are some of your likes, dislikes, talents, and challenges?
_____
_____
_____

▶ Which of your talents do you think is most important to you? Why? _____
_____
_____
_____
_____

▶ If you could change one thing about yourself, what would it be? Why? _____
_____
_____
_____
_____

▶ What did you discover about yourself that you hadn't realized before? _____
_____
_____
_____
_____

▶ Name three classmates and something you discovered about each of them that you didn't know before.
_____
_____
_____
_____

My Name

> **Objective:** Students will brainstorm and record adjectives to describe themselves and write an acrostic name poem using some of those adjectives.

Materials ▶
- thesaurus
- colored markers
- worksheet on page 18
- evaluation on page 19

Journal Starters ▶

I like my name because . . .
I do not like my name because . . .
Some people call me by my nickname which is . . .
If I could have any name I wanted, my name would be _____ because . . .

Visualization ▶

Encourage students to think of as many positive descriptive words that they can. Invite them to think of these words as cloth that can be made into the greatest set of clothes they can imagine. Ask students to imagine how great it would feel to wear these clothes.

Activity ▶

1. Before class, create an acrostic using your name to share with the students. Use colored markers to make it attractive and bright.

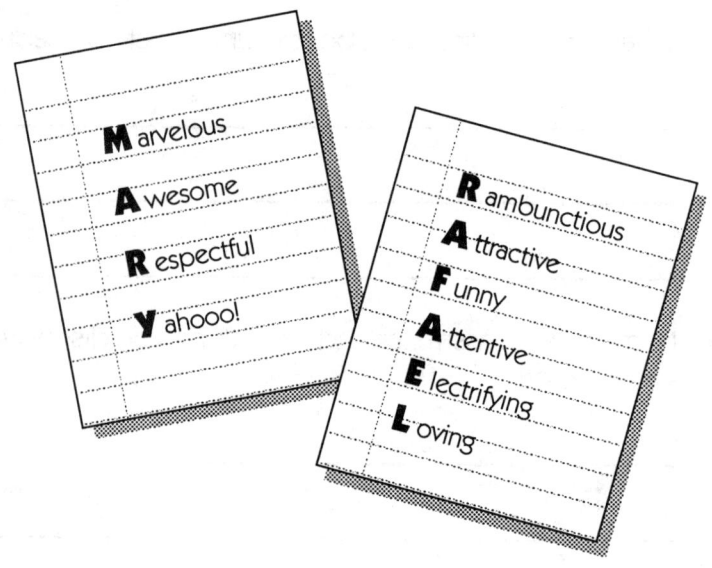

16 - Getting to Know Me

My Name

2. Brainstorm several positive adjectives for each letter of the alphabet with the entire class and record them on the board.

3. Distribute a copy of the worksheet on page 18 to each student. Encourage students to create acrostics from their names that describe who they are. Remind students that a thesaurus may be helpful as they brainstorm creative and interesting words.

4. Give students an opportunity to share their poems with the class. Students might also want to share any information they know about the history of their name, its meaning, or origin.

5. Encourage each student to complete the evaluation on page 19.

Getting to Know Me - 17

Name _____ Date _____

Name Poem

▶ Use the letters in your first and/or last name to create an acrostic poem. Be creative and think positively!

Name _____ Date _____

My Name

Evaluation

▶ Of all the words in your acrostic poem, which one best describes you?

Why? _____
_____
_____

▶ I like my name because _____
_____
_____
_____
_____

▶ I wouldn't want to change my name because _____
_____
_____
_____
_____

▶ Do you think you can tell something about a person by knowing just that person's name?

Why or why not? _____
_____
_____
_____

Wrap It Up

Objective: Students will learn more about themselves and their classmates by describing three items that are very important to them that reveal something about their qualities, traits, and interests.

Materials ▶
- evaluation on page 21

Journal Starters ▶

The best present I ever received was . . .
I really liked it because . . .
The best present I ever gave to anyone else was . . .
I knew it was special to that person because . . .

Visualization ▶

Encourage students to recall the best present they ever received. Why was it so special? Invite students to think about the best present they ever gave to anyone. Why was that present so special?

Activity ▶

1. Invite each student to think about three items that are very important to him or her. These items should reveal something about students, such as what they believe in, what they enjoy, or what they do best.
2. Have students collect the items from home and place them in a box. Invite students to wrap their boxes in gift wrap and bring them to school.
3. Give each student an opportunity to unwrap his or her box in front of the class and describe and explain each of the three items inside. Encourage students to share why they chose the items and what the items reveal about themselves.
4. Invite each student to complete the evaluation on page 21.

20 - Getting to Know Me

Name _____   Date _____

Wrap It Up

Evaluation

▶ If you wanted to tell a stranger about yourself and the only way you could communicate was to send a package with three items inside, what would you send? Explain what each item reveals about you.

_____
_____
_____
_____
_____

▶ Did anyone value the same item as you did? _____

What was it? _____

What do you and that person share in common? _____
_____
_____
_____

▶ Name three classmates and tell something you learned about each of them from the items they shared.

_____
_____
_____
_____
_____
_____
_____

Assets and Limitations

Objective: Students will evaluate their assets and limitations for the purpose of learning more about who they are.

Materials ▶
- worksheet on page 23
- evaluation on page 24

Journal Starters ▶
I define an asset as . . .
I define a limitation as . . .
I define a challenge as . . .
I define success as . . .

Visualization ▶ Encourage students to visualize themselves at the top of a ski slope. Invite them to think of themselves as top-ranked world skiers skiing in any event they wish. Encourage them to visualize what it would feel like to fly down the mountain with complete control achieving their best ski run ever.

Activity ▶
1. Create a transparency of the worksheet on page 23.
2. Discuss the definition of assets and limitations.
    - An asset can be something you like and do well, such as the talent to paint, the ability to ski well, or the ability to speak articulately.
    - A limitation can be something you do not like to do and/or do not do well, such as if you have difficulty playing the piano, are unable to sing, or are frightened of public speaking.
3. Survey yourself while inviting the students to listen as you think aloud and verbalize your thoughts. Modeling how to complete the worksheet will encourage students to respond to the worksheet openly and honestly.
4. Give each student a copy of the worksheet. Encourage students to respond as you guide them through each item. Invite students to use positive self-talk while completing the worksheet.
5. Invite each student to complete the evaluation on page 24.

22 - Getting to Know Me

Name _____ Date _____

Assets and Limitations Survey

▶ Complete the survey by writing an "A" beside each asset and an "L" beside each limitation. If you enjoy doing something and do it well, it is an asset. If you do not enjoy doing something or cannot do it well, it is a limitation. Be honest and answer as accurately as possible.

_____ 1. Reading

_____ 2. Writing

_____ 3. Solving math problems

_____ 4. Studying science

_____ 5. Giving and receiving presents

_____ 6. Cooking

_____ 7. Playing football

_____ 8. Participating in sports

_____ 9. Having a sense of humor

_____ 10. Working with children

_____ 11. Liking school

_____ 12. Fixing things and working with your hands

_____ 13. Helping people

_____ 14. Growing things

_____ 15. Being a good friend

_____ 16. Staying out of trouble

_____ 17. Exercising

_____ 18. Keeping up with current events

_____ 19. Working hard

_____ 20. Working with computers

_____ 21. Creating

_____ 22. Solving problems

_____ 23. Playing a musical instrument

_____ 24. Learn new things

_____ 25. Cleaning your room

_____ 26. Swimming

_____ 27. Sewing

_____ 28. Running

_____ 29. Singing

_____ 30. Sending and receiving letters

_____ 31. Taking care of myself

_____ 32. Being able to drive

_____ 33. Saving money

_____ 34. Liking myself

_____ 35. Being organized

Name _____ Date _____

Assets and Limitations

Evaluation

▶ Some of my assets are _____
_____
_____
_____

▶ Some of my limitations are _____
_____
_____
_____

▶ I feel _____ about my assets.

▶ I feel _____ about my limitations.

▶ I would like to change _____

   I can do this by _____
   _____

▶ It's okay that _____
   _____

▶ I am different from my friends because _____
   _____

▶ I would like to be able to _____

   I can do this by _____
   _____

Positive Thinking

Objective: Students will identify positive qualities about each other for the purpose of fostering positive thinking and a positive self-concept.

Materials ▶
- paper
- tape
- colored markers
- evaluation on page 26

Journal Starters ▶

Thinking positively is helpful because . . .
Thinking positively is difficult sometimes because . . .
When I know I am having negative thoughts, I . . .
I sometimes think negatively about myself when . . .

Visualization ▶

Encourage students to think of two negative issues in their lives. Invite them to visualize how they might change these issues from being negative to positive. Will they need to change how they think about the issues? What will they need to do?

Activity ▶

1. Brainstorm a list of positive comments and observations and then a list of negative comments and observations.
2. Discuss which list was easier to make. Why? Which list feels better?
3. Give each student a piece of paper and ask partners to help students tape the paper to their backs.
4. Give each student a different colored marker to write a positive comment about each person on the paper taped to his or her back.
5. After students have written comments, invite them to remove the paper from their backs and read the comments. Encourage students to comment on what their classmates wrote about them.
   - What comment did you like best? Why?
   - What comment didn't you like? Why?
   - Was it easy to think of a positive comment for everyone? Why or why not?
6. Invite each student to complete the evaluation on page 26.

Getting to Know Me - 25

Name _____ Date _____

Positive Thinking

Evaluation

▶ This activity was _____

because_____

_____

▶ I am glad that someone thought I am _____

▶ I really wonder why someone said I was _____

▶ I am glad that I told _____

that he/she was _____

because _____

_____

_____

▶ I think that I am _____

because _____

_____

_____

All About Me

Objective:
Students will create an amusing, fiction tale about themselves and then turn it into a story that reveals who they truly are and what they think.

Materials ▶
- worksheets on pages 28-30
- evaluation on page 31

Journal Starters ▶
I think that _____ is absurd because . . .
I _____ being absurd because . . .
If I wrote a story about myself, I would include . . .

Visualization ▶
Invite students to think about a time when they did something absurd, silly, or crazy. What did they do? What did others think? How did they feel?

Activity ▶
1. Divide students into pairs. Give each student a copy of the worksheet on page 28. Invite students to record their partner's zany answers when asked for a word that fits the category described on each line.
2. Give each student a copy of the worksheet on page 29. Have students transfer their zany words on the first worksheet into the corresponding blanks on the second worksheet to create a silly and amusing story about themselves.
3. Encourage students to read their absurd stories aloud to their partners.
4. Give each student a copy of the worksheet on page 30. This time, encourage students to fill in the blanks with true words that make sense and tell something about themselves.
5. Invite students to read their true stories aloud to the class.
6. Encourage students to compare the results of the absurd story with the true story.
7. Invite each student to complete the evaluation on page 31.

Getting to Know Me - 27

Name _____ Date _____

Zany Words

▶ Write down your partner's answers on each line. Encourage your partner to think of funny and zany words—the crazier the better.

1. Famous person's name _____
2. Adjective _____
3. Adjective _____
4. Zoo animal _____
5. School subject _____
6. Verb _____
7. Verb _____
8. Funny action _____
9. Animal home _____
10. Carnival ride _____
11. Verb _____
12. Name of sports star _____
13. Sound _____
14. Color _____
15. Verb _____
16. Emotion _____
17. Animal action _____
18. Verb _____
19. Something that makes noise _____
20. Time of day or night _____
21. Food _____
22. Occupation _____
23. Verb _____
24. Adjective _____
25. Emotion _____

Name _____ Date _____

How Absurd!

▶ Transfer your list of zany words to the corresponding blanks in the story below to create a zany, absurd tale.

My name is _____(1)_____ but my friends call me _____(2)_____.

Today I feel _____(3)_____. One of the things I think is special about me is my _____(4)_____. The thing that bothers me most about school is _____(5)_____. I'd rather _____(6)_____ than _____(7)_____.

I like teachers who _____(8)_____. My favorite place to be is in a _____(9)_____. One of the things that bothers me the most is my _____(10)_____. When I'm alone I like to _____(11)_____. The most important person in the world is _____(12)_____. Sometimes I like to listen to somebody _____(13)_____. I think the world should be _____(14)_____.

I think that families should _____(15)_____ together. I think that school should be a place where you feel _____(16)_____. I feel nervous when I'm asked to _____(17)_____. More than anything else, I like to _____(18)_____.

Sometimes I like to listen to a _____(19)_____. I get really angry when it's _____(20)_____. I feel proud when I have _____(21)_____. I wish that people would all be _____(22)_____ and I wish they wouldn't _____(23)_____. This year I hope I can become more _____(24)_____.

One thing that I'd like you to know about me is that I'm _____(25)_____.

Name _____ Date _____

A Story of Truth

▶ Fill in the blanks with truthful answers about who you are and the things you like. When you are finished, compare this story to the absurd story you created.

My name is _____ but my friends call me _____.

Today I feel _____. One of the things I think is special about me is my

_____. The thing that bothers me most about school is

_____. I'd rather _____ than _____.

I like teachers who _____. My favorite place to be is in a

_____. One of the things that bothers me the most is my

_____. When I'm alone I like to _____. The most

important person in the world is _____. Sometimes I like to listen to

somebody _____. I think the world should be _____.

I think that families should _____ together. I think that school should be a

place where you feel _____. I feel nervous when I'm asked to

_____. More than anything else, I like to _____.

Sometimes I like to listen to a _____. I get really angry when it's

_____. I feel proud when I have _____. I wish that

people would all be _____ and I wish they wouldn't

_____. This year I hope I can become more _____.

One thing that I'd like you to know about me is that I'm _____.

Name _____ Date _____

All About Me

Evaluation

▶ What did you think of your absurd story? _____
_____
_____

▶ Was it similar to the truthful story? _____

Why or why not? _____
_____
_____
_____

▶ I liked this activity because _____
_____
_____
_____

▶ Sometimes it's hard to tell the truth about myself because _____
_____
_____
_____

Getting to Know Me - 31

Laughing, Laughing, Laughing

Objective: Students will recognize the appropriate use of humor.

Materials ▶
- role play on page 33
- evaluation on page 34

Journal Starters ▶
Once I remember telling a funny story about . . . to my friends but no one laughed.
I think it is funny when . . . because . . .
I do not think it is funny when . . . because . . .

Visualization ▶
Encourage students to recall a time when they were with a group of peers and something funny happened. Ask them if anyone was insulted or hurt.

Activity ▶
1. Distribute copies of the role play and divide students into groups of three to rehearse.
2. After an appropriate amount of time, invite students to perform the role play.
3. After each group has performed, discuss how students felt as they played the various parts.
4. Invite each student to complete the evaluation on page 34.

Name _____   Date _____

It Isn't Funny

Role Play

Rehearse the following role play with your group. Discuss with your group members who will play which roles. You may want to rehearse the role play several times so everyone has a chance to play each role.

Actor 1

Sitting alone in the lunch room looking very unhappy and lonely having just broke up with a girl/boyfriend.

Actors 2 and 3

Walk into lunchroom together. They both notice Actor 1 sitting all alone and looking very sad but are unaware of the break up. All actors are great friends and often play practical jokes on each other. They decide to play a joke on Actor 1 and tease by saying that they saw Actor 1's girl/boyfriend with someone else. They think that this kind of humor might cheer up Actor 1. Both actors laugh wildly.

Actor 1

Gets angry, shouts, and runs off while Actors 2 and 3 stare at each other with a bewildered look wondering what they said that was so wrong.

Name _____   Date _____

Laughing, Laughing, Laughing

Evaluation

▶ In the role play, what did Actors 2 and 3 try to do to make Actor 1 feel better?
_____
_____
_____

▶ How do you think Actor 1 felt? Why? _____
_____
_____

▶ How do you think Actors 1's reaction made the other two feel? _____
_____
_____

▶ If you were Actor 2 or 3, what would you have done? Why? _____
_____
_____

▶ If you were Actor 1, what would you have done? Why? _____
_____
_____

▶ Has anything like this ever happened to you? _____

What happened? What did you do? _____
_____
_____

I Am the Color

Objective: Students will explore their emotions by relating them to color.

Materials ▶
- white art paper
- construction paper, fabric, and markers in various colors
- worksheet on page 36
- evaluation on page 37

Journal Starters ▶
My favorite color is . . . because . . .
The color . . . makes me think of . . .
When I wear my favorite color, I feel . . . because . . .
I like the colors . . . and . . . together because . . .
I do not like the color . . . because . . .

Visualization ▶ Invite students to close their eyes and visualize themselves wrapped in red. Ask students how they feel and what emotions may be associated with the color red. Repeat the visualization with other colors.

Activity ▶
1. Give each student a copy of the worksheet on page 36 and divide students into groups of three.
2. Encourage groups to discuss the colors and emotions and pair them up by assigning a color (or colors) to each emotion.
3. Invite each group to choose a color/emotion pair to create a role play around. Invite students to use construction paper, fabric, markers, and white art paper to create simple color props.
4. After an appropriate amount of time, invite the groups to perform their role plays with the whole class.
5. Discuss how colors reflect emotions.
6. Invite each student to complete the evaluation on page 37.

Controlling Emotions - 35

Name _____ Date _____

Emotions and Colors

▶ Write a color word on each blank to show which color(s) you think best represents each emotion.

Colors

red	purple	brown
orange	white	turquoise
yellow	black	pink
green	lavender	gold
blue	gray	silver

Emotions

angry _____ happy _____

anxious _____ hopeful _____

calm _____ jealous _____

confident _____ lonely _____

confused _____ nervous _____

depressed _____ peaceful _____

embarrassed _____ satisfied _____

excited _____ shy _____

grouchy _____ upset _____

Name _____ Date _____

I Am the Color

Evaluation

▶ What is your favorite color? _____

▶ Does the emotion you matched with this color accurately describe you? Explain.

_____
_____
_____

▶ Do you think colors are good indicators of emotion? _____

Why or why not? _____

_____
_____
_____

▶ Which emotion do you need to learn to control the most? _____

Why? _____

What can you do? _____

_____
_____
_____

Dealing with Anger

Objective: Students will recognize that there are several ways to deal with anger and identify which way they most often use.

Materials ▶
- worksheet on page 40
- evaluation on page 41

Journal Starters ▶

One thing that makes me really angry is . . .
When I get angry, I feel . . .
When I get angry, I react by . . .
I need to . . . when I get angry.

Visualization ▶

Encourage students to visualize a situation that would make them very angry. Invite them to think about who is with them, different ways they can react, and possible consequences.

Activity ▶

1. Discuss with students aggressive, assertive, and passive behavior.
    - Aggressive behavior can be characterized as forceful, sometimes irrational and confused, and impulsive.
    - Assertive behavior can be characterized as rational, firm, and straight-forward.
    - Passive behavior can be characterized as lacking direction and often shaped by outside influences.
2. Also, explain and give examples of the use of body language, facial expressions, and tone of voice.
3. Give each student a copy of the worksheet. Encourage students to complete it as openly and honestly as possible.

Dealing with Anger

4. After an appropriate amount of time, invite students to share and discuss their responses.
   - What triggered you to respond the way you did?
   - Were your responses aggressive, assertive, or passive?
   - Could the use of body language, facial expressions, and tone of voice affect how someone might interpret your responses and reactions?
   - Do you think your responses are the best possible? Why or why not?
   - Can you suggest other responses that would result in different reactions?
   - If you took more time to consider the consequences of your responses, would you have responded differently?

5. Discuss with students new techniques they may have learned to deal with anger. In addition, remind students of the importance of considering consequences before acting and ways to detect what triggers reactions.

6. Encourage each student to complete the evaluation on page 41.

Name _____ Date _____

Reaction Time

▶ As you read each situation below, record what your first reaction would be. Remember to be open and honest.

1. I had a bad day at school. As soon as I got home, someone yelled at me.
   _____

2. I thought I was doing better in school until my teacher told me that I was failing.
   _____

3. My brother took my favorite tape and lost it. _____
   _____

4. Another student took some of my food at lunch. _____
   _____

5. My friend blamed me for something I didn't do. _____
   _____

6. My mom/dad said that we'd do something together but she/he took off without me.
   _____

7. My parents won't let me go to the concert. _____
   _____

8. My friends think that I am talking behind their backs. _____
   _____

9. Some kid keeps pushing me in the hall. _____
   _____

Name _____ Date _____

Dealing with Anger

Evaluation

▶ When I choose to take my anger out on someone, I _____
_____
_____

▶ I feel _____ when I do this because _____
_____
_____

▶ When I choose to deal with my anger in a physical way, I _____
_____
_____

▶ I think that I could deal better with my anger by _____
_____
_____

▶ I want to tell the members of my family that _____
_____
_____

▶ I want to tell my teachers _____
_____

▶ When people are upset with me, I would like them to tell me _____
_____
_____

Should I Tell the Truth?

Objective: Students will develop skills to help them make good choices in difficult situations.

Materials ▶
- role play on page 43
- evaluation on page 44

Journal Starters ▶

One of the most difficult choices I ever made was . . .
It was difficult because . . .
When I had to make this choice I . . .

Visualization ▶

Encourage students to visualize a time when they were presented with a choice and were proud of the choice that they made. Invite them to visualize how they made that choice. Ask them to think about how the situation might have changed if they had made another choice.

Activity ▶

1. Give each student a copy of the role play.
2. Divide students into groups of four to rehearse.
3. After an appropriate amount of rehearsal time, invite the groups to perform the role play.
4. After all groups have had the opportunity to perform, discuss how students felt as they played the various roles.
    - How did it make you feel knowing the complete truth was not told? Did you feel disloyal?
    - How do you think you would feel if you told the truth?
    - Can you describe a time when this happened to you? What happened? How did you feel?
5. Invite each student to complete the evaluation on page 44.

42 - Making Wise Choices

Telling the Truth

Role Play

Actors 1, 2, 3, and store owner

Three friends (Actors 1, 2, and 3) decide to skip school. During their day of adventure, Actor 1 secretly thinks about a plan to get a free candy bar. The three friends go to a store where Actor 1 slips a candy bar into Actor 2's pocket. Actor 2 has no idea what is happening but Actor 3 sees everything. As the three friends are leaving the store, the store owner begins to question the three friends and finds the candy bar in Actor 2's pocket. The store owner allows Actors 1 and 3 to leave but demands that Actor 2 stay and face the consequences of stealing.

Outside the store, Actor 3 confronts Actor 1 about slipping the candy bar into Actor 2's pocket. But, Actor 1 will not confess to the truth because of the trouble he or she could get into. Actor 1 thinks that Actor 2's parents won't be as angry, so it is better if Actor 2 takes the blame. Actor 3 tries very hard to persuade Actor 1 to tell the truth but Actor 1 will not listen. Actor 3 doesn't know what to do but begins to verbalize some of the options and their consequences.

Name _____ Date _____

Should I Tell the Truth?

Evaluation

▶ What is Actor 3's dilemma? _____
_____
_____

▶ What will happen if Actor 3 does not tell the truth? How will he or she feel?
_____
_____
_____

▶ What will happen if Actor 3 does tells the truth? _____
_____
_____
_____

▶ If you were Actor 3, what would you do? Why? _____
_____
_____
_____
_____

▶ Have you ever been in a similar situation? Explain. _____
_____
_____
_____

Is It Real?

Objective: Students will learn to discern between reality and fantasy for the purpose of learning to make wise choices and gaining a better understanding of themselves.

Materials ▶
- overhead projector
- worksheet on page 46
- evaluation on page 47

Journal Starters ▶
I believe that . . .
I know that . . .
It is absolutely true that . . .
I used to believe that . . . but now I know that . . .
Although some people think so, it is not true that . . .

Visualization ▶ Invite students to visualize themselves on the top of a mountain on a hot summer day. The sky is a brilliant blue. The breeze is cool and refreshing and they feel free and strong. The climb to the top was difficult and filled with obstacles. Encourage students to think about the obstacles and how they dealt with them.

Activity ▶
1. Create a transparency of the worksheet.
2. Give each student a copy of the worksheet. Encourage students to complete it openly and honestly.
3. After an appropriate amount of time, invite students to share their responses while recording them on the transparency.
4. Invite each student to complete the evaluation on page 47.

Making Wise Choices

Name _____ Date _____

Real or Fantasy?

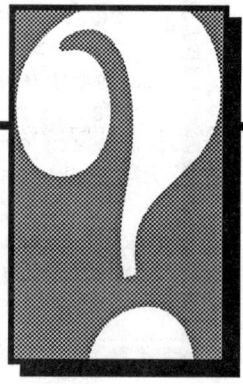

▶ Record whether you think each statement is real or fantasy by placing a mark under the appropriate column. Your answers may be different from someone else's answers. Do your own thinking and remember to answer honestly.

	Real	Fantasy
1. The moon is made of green Swiss cheese.	_____	_____
2. People die.	_____	_____
3. The halls are noisier when a weather change is on its way.	_____	_____
4. Everyone loves chocolate.	_____	_____
5. Advertisements are always true.	_____	_____
6. Anyone can get straight A's.	_____	_____
7. It's a good idea to believe what you read.	_____	_____
8. Cigarettes won't hurt you.	_____	_____
9. If you like yourself then you can change.	_____	_____
10. People who like themselves are not afraid to take risks.	_____	_____
11. It's okay if I fail.	_____	_____
12. I know I can't do everything.	_____	_____
13. People come from different planets.	_____	_____
14. If I see an educational film, I know all the information is correct.	_____	_____
15. My best friend is a good person.	_____	_____
16. I can have everything I want.	_____	_____
17. Life is made up of choices.	_____	_____
18. I can control what happens to me.	_____	_____

Name _____ Date _____

Is It Real?

Evaluation

▶ I know that what I consider real may be different from what my friends consider real because _____
_____
_____
_____

▶ What are five things you used to believe were real which you now know are fantasy?
_____
_____
_____
_____

▶ Why do you think fantasy is sometimes perceived as being real? _____
_____
_____
_____
_____

Decision-Making Skills

Objective: Students will learn the steps involved in decision-making for the purpose of applying the skills to their real-life situations.

Materials ▶
- overhead projector
- worksheet on page 50
- evaluation on page 51

Journal Starters ▶ When my friends ask me to do something and I want to do something else, I . . .

I make decisions by . . .

Visualization ▶ Invite students to visualize themselves being faced with a decision. Perhaps they have a choice between two weekend outings or need to choose a science project topic. Encourage students to think about how they make decisions and what factors help them decide.

Activity ▶
1. Create a transparency of the worksheet. Discuss the acronym for the steps in the decision-making process.

   Determine all possible choices presented by the situation.
   Evaluate and brainstorm all possible solutions.
   Choose a solution that makes sense to you.
   Identify with it! Visualize the outcome.
   Develop a plan and a schedule to follow.
   Examine the outcome of the plan and decision. Celebrate success!

2. Brainstorm scenarios from students' personal lives that can be used in role plays.
3. Select one of the scenarios and model making a decision. Be sure to verbalize your thinking. Encourage students to ask questions as you progress through the steps.
4. Divide the class into pairs. Invite students to write a role play using one of the scenarios and demonstrating the decision-making steps.

Decision-Making Skills

5. After an appropriate amount of time, invite students to perform their role plays.

6. Invite students to discuss each others' scenarios and the decision-making steps they used.
   - Do you think there could be other choices?
   - Are there any other solutions that make sense?
   - Can the plan be implemented without too much stress?
   - Is that outcome realistic? Can you honestly identify with it?

7. Invite each student to complete the evaluation on page 51.

Name _____ Date _____

DECIDE

▶ Identify which step in the decision-making process is represented by each statement below by placing the appropriate number in each blank.

1. **D**etermine all possible choices presented by the situation.
2. **E**valuate all possible solutions.
3. **C**hoose a solution that makes sense to you.
4. **I**dentify with it! Visualize the outcome.
5. **D**evelop a plan and a schedule to follow.
6. **E**xamine the outcome of the plan and decision. Celebrate success!

_____ After looking at all of these ideas, I realize that there are several silly ones. There are also several over which I have no control.

_____ It looks like I have two choices. Do I want to go out for hamburgers or do I want to save my money for that stereo?

_____ I have thought this solution through to the end and I can now see what I have to do to make it work!

_____ The solution I decided to act on worked. I wonder if there are other things I could have chosen which might have worked better. There was one outcome I didn't enjoy. Next time I might try another approach.

_____ I've made a choice and so now I will make a list of what I need to do to make my plan work.

_____ I really appreciate you helping me think of all the possibilities. Now I have several possible solutions from which to choose.

_____ This idea looks like it might work. I think I will try this one.

50 - Making Wise Choices

Name _____ Date _____

Decision-Making Skills

Evaluation

▶ Describe the last situation in which you had to make a decision.
_____
_____
_____
_____
_____

▶ How did your decision turn out? _____
_____
_____
_____

▶ Would you make a different choice if you had to do it again? Explain. _____
_____
_____
_____

▶ Which step in the decision-making process is most difficult for you? Why? _____
_____
_____
_____

The Art of Refusing

Objective: Students will learn the steps involved in refusing for the purpose of applying the skills to their real-life situations.

Materials ▶
- overhead projector
- worksheet on page 54
- evaluation on page 55

Journal Starters ▶

When my friends ask me to do something I do not want to do, I . . .
I may refuse to do something by . . .
It is sometimes hard to refuse because . . .

Visualization ▶

Invite students to visualize themselves with a group of friends. Your friends want to play a practical joke on another student and are planning what they will do. You do not want to be a part of it because you know it will most likely end up hurting the other student. You know, however, if you don't play along, your friends will make fun of you. What will you do? How can you refuse?

Activity ▶

1. Create a transparency of the worksheet on page 54. Discuss the acronym for the refusal-making process.

   R eally ask questions about the activity.
   E xamine all of the consequences.
   F ind alternatives. Suggest different things to do.
   U se persuasion. Be assertive.
   S tate all of the consequences and problems.
   E xit from the situation and leave doors open.
   No ultimatums.

2. Brainstorm scenarios from students' personal lives that can be used in role plays.

3. Select one of the scenarios and model the refusal-making process steps. Be sure to verbalize your thinking. Encourage students to ask questions as you progress through the refusal steps.

The Art of Refusing

4. Divide the class into pairs. Invite students to write role plays using one of the scenarios and demonstrating the refusal steps.

5. After an appropriate amount of time, invite students to perform their role plays.

6. Invite students to discuss each others' scenarios and the refusal-making steps they used.
    - Do you think there could be other problems or consequences?
    - Are there any other alternatives that make sense?
    - Could you have been more assertive or less assertive?
    - Were doors left open? Did you give an ultimatum?

7. Invite each student to complete the evaluation on page 55.

Making Wise Choices - 53

Name _____ Date _____

REFUSE

▶ Identify which step in the refusal-making process is represented by each statement below by placing the appropriate number in each blank.

1. **R**eally ask questions about the activity.
2. **E**xamine all of the consequences.
3. **F**ind alternatives! Suggest different things to do. Present these.
4. **U**se persuasion. Be assertive!
5. **S**tate all of the consequences and problems.
6. **E**xit from situation and leave doors open. No ultimatums.

▶ John is trying to convince Rick that they should take the beer his parents bought and find a car to go joy riding. Rick's response could include any of the following.

_____ Why do you want to do that? Do you really think we could get away with it?

_____ I really think that I would rather go to the mall and hang around. I'll probably get something to eat and then go see that new movie. I hope I see you there.

_____ You know, John, I heard Cindy say that she was going to the mall to hang out with her friends. I was thinking maybe we could check it out.

_____ You know, we could end up in a lot of trouble. We could get stopped by the police or get caught by your parents.

54 - Making Wise Choices

Name _____ Date _____

The Art of Refusing

Evaluation

▶ Describe a situation in which you knew you should refuse but didn't know quite how to handle it.

_____
_____
_____
_____

▶ What will you try to do the next time you are faced with a similar situation? _____

_____
_____
_____
_____

▶ Which strategy in the REFUSE steps works best for you? Why? _____

_____
_____
_____

It's All About Change

> **Objective:** Students will consider how they deal with change and new situations for the purpose of improving their coping and decision-making strategies.

Materials ▶
- role play on page 57
- evaluation on page 58

Journal Starters ▶

When I am faced with a new situation, I . . .

I feel _____ when I have to change because . . .

Visualization ▶

Encourage students to picture themselves in a new and difficult situation requiring them to change in some way. Invite them to visualize what they must do to cope.

Activity ▶

1. Give each student a copy of the role play on page 57.
2. Divide students into threes to rehearse.
3. After an appropriate amount of rehearsal time, invite groups to perform the role play.
4. After each group has the opportunity to perform, discuss how students felt as they played the various roles.
   - How do you feel when you are presented with a difficult situation requiring you to make some changes?
   - Can you describe a time when you did not make any changes and fought the new situation? What happened? How did you feel?
   - Can you name some circumstances that would involve making a decision to change your attitude or behavior to cope with the new situation?
5. Encourage each student to complete the evaluation on page 58.

56 - Making Wise Choices

Name _____ Date _____

Dealing with Change

Role Play

Choose a role to play and rehearse the scene with your group members.

Actor 1

You are the youngest of five children and have always lived in the city with your family and have never been away from them. One of your sisters is very sick and your family will be at the hospital most of the time. Because of this, your parents have decided for you to stay with your aunt and uncle on their ranch in the country. You have never met your aunt and uncle before. You have a choice—accept this change or fight it. After Actors 2 and 3 have explained their expectations, you go outside and work through your feelings about the situation. You finally decide that it will be best to learn all that you can and to help your aunt and uncle out as much as possible.

Actor 2

You are Actor 1's aunt. You expect Actor 1 to obey very strict rules while staying at your ranch. You expect Actor 1 to be home at a certain time, do homework promptly, and do chores around the ranch.

Actor 3

You are Actor 1's uncle. You are hard-working and expect Actor 1 to work hard as well. You explain many of the ranch chores and outline your expectations to Actor 1.

Name _____ Date _____

It's All About Change

Evaluation

▶ How did Actor 1 first feel about the situation? _____
_____
_____

▶ Why do you think Actor 1 decided to adjust to the situation instead of fighting it?
_____
_____
_____

▶ What do you think would have happened if Actor 1 had chosen not to change?
_____
_____
_____

▶ If you were in a similar situation, what would you have done? Why? _____
_____
_____
_____

▶ Tell about a time that you had to adjust to a new situation. Explain how you felt and what you decided to do.
_____
_____
_____

Are You Prepared?

> **Objective:**
> Students will recognize the need to be organized and responsible for themselves and determine one way they can become more organized and responsible.

Materials ▶
- role play on page 60
- evaluation on page 61

Journal Starters ▶
I am organized when I . . . because . . .
I am responsible when I . . . because . . .
The hardest time for me to be organized is when . . .
I am most irresponsible when . . .

Visualization ▶ Encourage students to visualize a very important competition in which they have been invited to participate. Invite students to close their eyes and visualize what they must do to prepare. Remind students that if they are not prepared or have forgotten to bring something, they will not have the opportunity to compete.

Activity ▶
1. Give each student a copy of the role play on page 60. Divide students into pairs to rehearse the role play.
2. After an appropriate rehearsal time, invite pairs to perform the role play.
3. After each pair has had the opportunity to perform, discuss how students felt as they dramatized the scene and related the characters' situations to their own experiences.
   - How do you feel when you are running late and are not organized for the day?
   - How do you feel when you are organized and on time?
   - Can you describe a time when you were not responsible? What happened? How did you feel?
   - What are some characteristics of an organized person?
   - What are some characteristics of a responsible person?
4. Invite each student to complete the evaluation on page 61.

Taking Responsibility - 59

Name _____ Date _____

The Day Begins

Role Play

Choose a role and rehearse the scene described with your partner.

Actor 1

You wake up on time. After taking a shower and brushing your teeth, you dress in the clothes that you chose the night before. You have plenty of time to eat a healthy breakfast. All of your homework was completed the night before and your books are laid out in a special place by the front door. You made sure that your permission slip was signed the night before and you have plenty of time to walk leisurely to your bus stop. You are happy and relaxed as you leave for school.

Actor 2

You wake up late and can't find anything to wear. You are frustrated because you feel like you might miss your bus to school. You didn't finish your homework and can't find your math book. You have to skip breakfast to make up time. As you frantically run to catch the bus, you realize that you forgot your lunch money and permission slip. You are angry when you get on the bus and you yell at your best friend.

Name _____ Date _____

Are You Prepared?

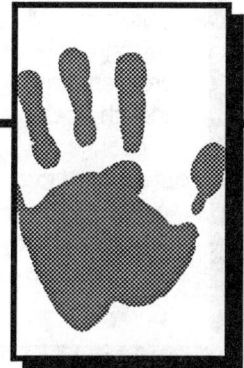

Evaluation

▶ In the role play, how did Actor 1 take care of him or herself?
_____
_____
_____

▶ What did Actor 2 do? _____
_____
_____

▶ Who do you think had a better day at school that day? Why? _____
_____
_____
_____

▶ Are you more like Actor 1 or Actor 2? Why? _____
_____
_____
_____

▶ What is one thing you could do to be more responsible for taking care of yourself?
_____
_____
_____

I Was Involved

> **Objective:**
> Students will recognize how problem-solving and choices can change the outcome of events and how to be more responsible for their own actions.

Materials ▶
- overhead projector
- writing paper
- pencils
- role play on page 63
- evaluation on page 64

Journal Starters ▶
I once was asked to . . .by my friend.
I felt . . .when he/she asked me.
I decided to . . . because . . .
I made the decision to . . .because . . .

Visualization ▶
Invite students to visualize being with a group of friends. One friend shows you a copy of the math exam that he or she took from the teacher's desk. This friend wants to hide the stolen exam in your locker. How do you feel? What do you want to do? What do you decide to do? How does your decision make you feel?

Activity ▶
1. Give each student a copy of the role play to read.
2. Brainstorm different solutions to the problem and record the solutions on the overhead projector.
3. Divide students into groups of three or four and invite them to create and rehearse a role play using one of the solutions.
4. After an appropriate amount of time, invite groups to perform the role play.
5. After each group has had the opportunity to perform, discuss how students felt as they dramatized the scene and related to the characters' experiences.
   - Do you think your solution was the best one? Why or why not?
   - If you were in the same situation, what would you do? Why?
   - Have you every been in a situation similar to this? What happened?
6. Invite each student to complete the evaluation on page 64.

Name _____   Date _____

Secrets and Silence

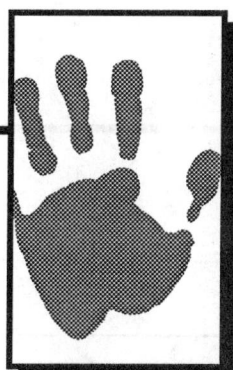

Role Play

Write a solution to this role play and rehearse it with your partners.

Actors 1, 2, and 3

Actor 1 tells Actors 2 and 3 some very personal and confidential things about him or herself. Later, Actors 2 and 3 tell other students what Actor 1 told them in confidence.

Actor 1

You are upset with your two friends (Actors 2 and 3) because it seems the whole school now knows about the things you told your friends in confidence. You confront Actors 2 and 3 and tell them that they have violated your trust by telling things you told them in private.

Actor 2

You know that you and Actor 3 did in fact tell some personal things about Actor 1 to other students at school but you don't want to admit it to Actor 1 because it may ruin your friendship. You don't want to lose Actor 1 as a friend so you consider blaming the whole incident on Actor 3. But you also consider taking responsibility for your actions by confessing to what you have done, leaving Actor 3 out of it, and hoping that Actor 1 will accept your apology. There are several options and you are not sure which one to choose.

Name _____ Date _____

I Was Involved

Evaluation

▶ How did Actor 1 feel? _____
_____
_____

▶ How did Actor 2 feel? _____
_____
_____

▶ What was the decision that Actor 2 had to make? _____
_____
_____

▶ What would you do if your were Actor 2? Why? _____
_____
_____

▶ Of all the solutions presented, which one do you think was the best? Why?
_____
_____

▶ Has anything similar ever happened to you? What happened? What did you do?
_____
_____
_____

"Cop Outs"

Objective: Students will identify excuses and rationalizations or "cop outs" in order to learn the value in taking responsibility for their actions.

Materials ▶
- scissors
- tape or glue
- art paper
- worksheets on pages 66-67
- evaluation on page 68

Journal Starters ▶

Sometimes when I'm in trouble, I try to get out of it by . . .
Once I said . . . when the truth was really . . .
When I come up with excuses I feel . . .

Visualization ▶

Encourage students to think about a time when they made up an excuse to avoid a negative consequence. How did they feel? Encourage students to think of a time when they accepted responsibility for their actions. How did they feel?

Activity ▶

1. Divide students into groups of three.
2. Give each group a copy of each worksheet, scissors, and glue or tape.
3. Invite groups to cut out the statements from both worksheets.
4. Encourage students to work as a group to match each responsible statement with the corresponding "cop out" statement.
5. Students can glue the paired statements on a sheet of art paper.
6. Use group discussion to examine the merits of taking responsibility for actions rather than copping out.
    - What makes a statement a "cop out?" Why?
    - Which statements ("cop out" or responsible) do you think are better? Why?
    - Have you ever used either type of statement before? What happened?
7. Invite each student to complete the evaluation on page 68.

Taking Responsibility - 65

Name _____   Date _____

Responsible Statements

▶ Cut out the responsible statements and pair them with a "cop out" statement.

I noticed that the house needed to be cleaned.
I pay attention to the rules and follow them.
Turning the money in is the right thing to do.
I need to listen to the teacher and follow instructions so I don't miss lunch.
I forgot to watch the news. I needed to tell Mom about the assignment.
I didn't put my homework away in the proper place.
I chose to pay attention to an argument my parents had. It had nothing to do with me.
I know I should not take things that don't belong to me.
I can make my own decisions. I don't need to do drugs.
I chose to skip class. My friend did not coerce me.
I can do what is right. I will not lie for my brother.

Name _____ Date _____

"Cop Out" Statements

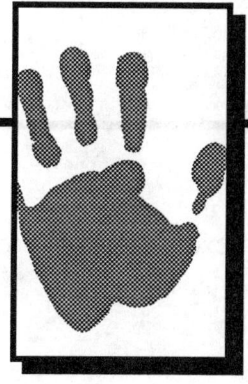

▶ Cut out the "cop out" statements and pair them with a responsible statement.

My sister threw my homework away.
He made me skip class.
My friend wanted me to take drugs.
My brother told me to lie for him.
The money was just sitting there so I took it.
You never told me that rule.
The store shouldn't have left the tape sitting right there on the counter.
My mom didn't let me watch the news for my homework assignment.
The teacher kept me in during lunch.
Mom didn't say I had to clean the house.
My parents were fighting so I didn't do my homework.

Taking Responsibility - 67

Name _____ Date _____

"Cop Outs"

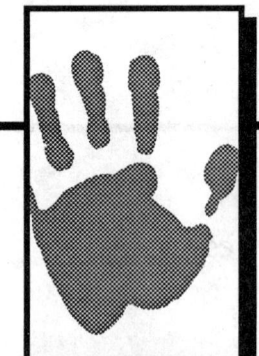

Evaluation

▶ Have you ever been in a situation where you made an excuse in order to avoid a negative consequence? What happened?
_____
_____
_____
_____

▶ If you were faced with the same situation again, would you do the same thing? Why or why not?
_____
_____
_____

▶ Is it easier to make responsible statements or "cop outs?" Why?_____
_____
_____
_____

▶ Do you think it is better to face the consequences by taking responsibility for your actions or to make excuses and avoid any negative consequences? Why?
_____
_____
_____
_____

Accept Responsibility

> **Objective:**
> Students will identify excuses and rationalizations or "cop outs" and change them into responsible statements to learn the value of taking responsibility for their actions.

Materials ▶
- worksheet on page 70
- evaluation on page 71

Journal Starters ▶
When I accept responsibility for my behavior, I . . .
I felt . . . when this happened because . . .

Visualization ▶
Encourage students to visualize themselves as a supervisor on a job. What are the qualities you would want in a supervisor? Remind them that they must set a good example for the other employees, such as assuming responsibility for mistakes. Could you be this kind of supervisor?

Activity ▶
1. Review with students the difference between "cop outs" and responsible statements.
2. Give each student a copy of the worksheet on page 70. Invite students to transform each "cop out" into a responsible statement.
3. After an appropriate amount of time, encourage students to share and discuss their answers.
   - What makes the statement a "cop out" or responsible statement? Why?
   - Which statement ("cop out" or responsible) do you think is better? Why?
   - Have you ever used either statement before? What happened?
4. Invite each student to complete the evaluation on page 71.

Name _____ Date _____

A Positive Change

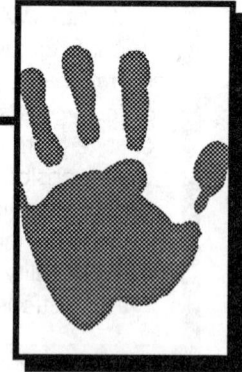

▶ Write a "C" beside each "cop out" statement and an "R" beside each responsible statement. On the back of this paper, change each "cop out" into a responsible statement.

_____ 1. There isn't enough time!

_____ 2. If they would just leave me alone, I could get everything done.

_____ 3. I needed to call those people earlier last night.

_____ 4. My mother didn't tell me to do it.

_____ 5. You were supposed to help me!

_____ 6. I thought that Ms. Haynes took care of those lists.

_____ 7. I need to schedule my time better.

_____ 8. None of this would have happened if my brother didn't do that.

_____ 9. They should have called to remind me.

_____ 10. If I was better organized, no one would need to put a note in my box.

_____ 11. I need to be more careful about what I tell my friends.

_____ 12. I forgot to write it down on my calendar.

Name _____ Date _____

Accept Responsibility

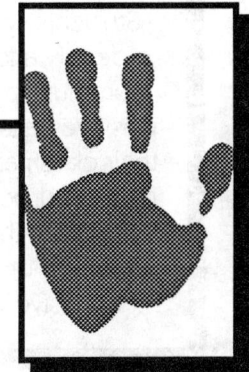

Evaluation

▶ Do you find it easier to assume responsibility for your actions or to make excuses? Why?

_____
_____
_____
_____

▶ How can you change a "cop out" into a responsible statement? _____

_____
_____
_____

▶ Name one "cop out" you used most recently and then change it to a responsible statement.

_____
_____
_____

▶ What have you learned about assuming responsibility for your actions? _____

_____
_____
_____

How Others See Me

> **Objective:** Students will identify and communicate positive traits in their classmates for the purpose of making the group more cohesive.

Materials ▶
- worksheet on page 73
- evaluation on page 74

Journal Starter ▶

I can show other people that they are worthwhile by . . .
It is important to be honest with others so that . . .
By being honest and positive with others, I . . .
I like it when people tell me . . . because . . .

Visualization ▶

Encourage students to visualize a place where people concentrate on the positive and say honest and positive things to each other. Invite students to think about how an environment like this would feel if it were at home, at school, or in the community.

Activity ▶

1. Divide students into groups of five and assign a group leader.
2. Give each student a copy of the worksheet on page 73. Remind students to think positively as they complete the worksheet.
3. Have students cut their statements apart after they have written them and give them to the group leader. The group leader can distribute the comments to the appropriate students.
4. Encourage students to read the comments written by others in their group. Invite students to express how the positive comments they received made them feel.
5. Invite each student to complete the evaluation on page 74.

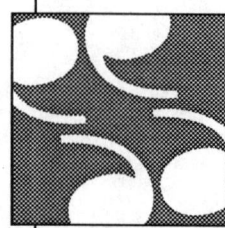

72 - Improving Communication

Name _____ Date _____

Positive Feedback

▶ Write the names of the members in your group in the boxes provided below. Write a positive statement next to each person's name. Remember to be kind, complimentary, and sincere. Then cut the statements apart and give them to your group leader.

Name	Comment
Name	Comment
Name	Comment
Name	Comment

Improving Communication - 73

Name _____ Date _____

How Others See Me

Evaluation

▶ I feel good because someone thinks that _____
_____
_____

▶ I am surprised because someone said _____
_____
_____

▶ I wish someone had said _____
_____
_____

▶ The positive comments I made to my group members probably made them feel _____
_____
_____

Cooperative Effort

Objective: Students will recognize the need for good communication to work cooperatively.

Materials ▶
- writing paper and art paper
- pens and colored markers
- evaluation on page 76

Journal Starters ▶

When I work with someone else, I . . .
I like (or do not like) to . . . with others.
The best part about working with others is . . .
The worst thing about working with others is . . .

Visualization ▶

Encourage students to visualize themselves flying in formation high above the earth with six other pilots—turning, diving, and in complete synchronization with the other airplanes. Every turn, every dip, every movement is mirrored over and over again. Think of the patterns. Imagine the possibilities.

Activity ▶

1. As a whole group, brainstorm ideas for a short story, poem, or advertisement.
2. Divide students into pairs. Invite pairs to choose a short story, poem, or advertisement to write and illustrate using ideas from the brainstorming session.
3. Before beginning, encourage each pair to cooperatively decide which partner will do the writing for the project and which one will illustrate.
4. After an appropriate amount of time, invite students to share their writing and illustrations.
5. Discuss how students felt about the activity.
   - How did you decide who would do what?
   - How did you come to agreement on the type of writing—story, poem, or advertisement?
   - How did you decide the theme?
   - Was it easy to work with your partner? Why or why not? How did you feel about the process?
   - What role did clear communication play in your joint effort to complete a project?
6. Encourage each student to complete the evaluation on page 76.

Improving Communication - 75

Name _____ Date _____

Cooperative Effort

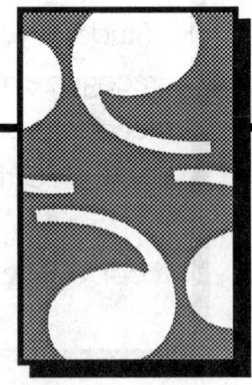

Evaluation

▶ It is easy to work with someone else because _____
_____
_____

▶ It is difficult to work with someone else because _____
_____
_____

▶ When I work with someone I need to _____
_____
_____

▶ I wish I had been able to _____
_____
_____

▶ I think that the activity would have been better if _____
_____
_____

▶ My partner and I communicated best when we _____
_____
_____

Communication Clues

Objective:
Students will learn to identify and understand various types of body language and behavior to better understand how these communication clues affect relationships.

Materials ▶
- role plays on pages 79-80
- evaluation on page 81

Journal Starters ▶
I think communication is . . .
I think assertive behavior is . . .
I think aggressive behavior is . . .
I think passive behavior is . . .
I use body language when I want to communicate . . .

Visualization ▶
Invite students to close their eyes and visualize an environment where all communication is done non-verbally. Encourage students to visual a person's facial expression and body language if he or she is angry. Have students visual the non-verbal communication for other emotions as well.

Activity ▶
1. Discuss the following concepts with students.
    - Communication is information passed by a sender to a receiver. The process can include verbal and non-verbal clues.
    - *Assertive* communication is usually clear, firm, and rational.
    - *Aggressive* communication is often delivered with anger, confusion, and irrational thinking. Non-verbal clues do not always support the verbal communication.
    - *Passive* communication is often shaped by outside influences. The communicator is often directed by situations rather than taking charge of the events and circumstances.
    - Non-verbal clues communicate information through the use of body language, facial expressions, and tone of voice.
2. Copy the role plays on pages 79-80 onto sturdy, colorful paper and cut the cards apart.

Improving Communication - 77

Communication Clues

3. Divide students into groups of three or four. Give each group a card with one role-play scenario on it. Encourage students to write and rehearse role plays with aggressive, assertive, and passive responses to the described scenario.

4. After an appropriate amount of time, invite groups to perform their role plays.

5. Discuss how the responses were interpreted.
   - Did the actors give clear messages? Were the verbal and non-verbal clues similar?
   - Did the actors give mixed messages? Were the verbal and non-verbal clues different?
   - What are the benefits of giving clear messages?
   - What problems can arise from mixed messages?
   - Could you identify a difference between assertive, aggressive, and passive responses?

6. Invite each student to complete the evaluation on page 81.

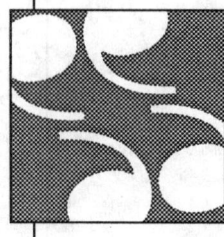

Name _____ Date _____

How Will You Respond?

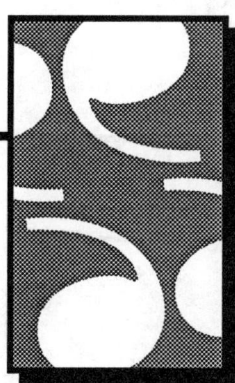

Role Plays

Your teacher tells you that she will not accept the paper you honestly forgot at home. She will not even accept it late. What will you say?

Your boss tells you that you have to work on Saturday. You agree but in the back of your mind you are thinking about the fact that you already made plans to spend the day at the mall with your friends. How will your response to your boss look and sound?

Your best friend has made plans with you for Saturday. He now wants to cancel and spend the day going skiing with someone else. How will you react? What words will you use? What body language will you use?

At the last minute, your mom changes her mind about your being able to go to the movies with your friends. She wants you to stay home and babysit. What will your response be to your mom?

Name _____ Date _____

How Will You Respond?

Role Plays

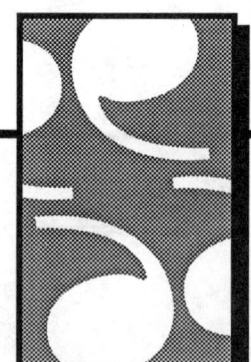

Your friend took things from the classroom. You know he did it but you are getting the blame. He won't tell the truth. What might your body language tell those around you?

The person sitting with you at lunch takes your dessert. You know the person took it, but you can't prove it. How will you react—verbally or non-verbally?

Your friend has been telling stories behind your back. These stories are spreading all around school. How will you communicate your feelings?

You are asked to get off the bus because you wouldn't follow the driver's instructions. How will you react as you leave the bus? What will you do? What will you say?

Name _____ Date _____

Communication Clues

Evaluation

▶ Assertive communication is _____
_____
_____

▶ Aggressive communication is _____
_____
_____
_____

▶ Passive communication is _____
_____
_____

▶ This activity taught me that when I communicate with someone I need to _____
_____
_____
_____

▶ It is important that my verbal and non-verbal communication are similar because _____
_____
_____
_____

Listen to Me

> **Objective:** Students will recognize the benefit of communicating to resolve conflict.

Materials ▶
- overhead projector
- worksheet on page 83
- evaluation on page 84

Journal Starters ▶ When my family is faced with a problem or conflict, we . . .
When my friends and I are faced with a problem, we . . .
When I am faced with a problem, I . . . because . . .

Visualization ▶ Invite students to visualize themselves floating in a small boat on a river holding on to a rope from the dock. Tell them to think about letting go. What will happen? Relate the feeling to not having all the facts about a situation, over reacting or misinterpreting, and as a result "drifting" far from the true story.

Activity ▶
1. Give each student a copy of the worksheet to complete.
2. After an appropriate amount of time, encourage students to share their responses. Record their answers on the overhead projector, so the class can pick the three best solutions.
3. Divide students into groups of three to write and rehearse a role play using one of the three solutions.
4. After the groups have finished rehearsing, invite them to perform their role plays. Discuss how students felt as they dramatized the scenes and related to the characters' situations.
    - Do you think the response you performed in your role play was the best possible? Why or why not?
    - Can you describe a time you were in a similar situation? What happened? How did you feel?
    - Do you think people react more wisely if they take time to think and discuss the circumstances? Why or why not?
5. Encourage each student to complete the evaluation on page 84.

Name _____ Date _____

Conflict Resolution

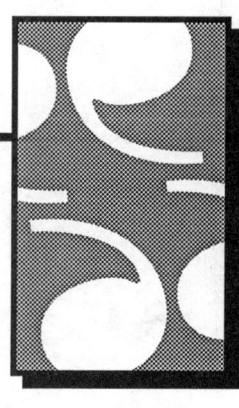

▶ Your parents are very upset about the reports they have received from your teachers, so they are restricting you for the next six weeks. Your older brother is always picking on you. When you fight, you find it very hard to concentrate on your homework. On top of all of this, you are finding it hard to tell your parents all the things that are bothering you.

▶ What are three ways you can communicate your feelings about this situation?

_____
_____
_____
_____
_____

▶ For each of the three different approaches, what are some possible responses from your parents.

_____
_____
_____
_____
_____

Name _____ Date _____

Listen to Me

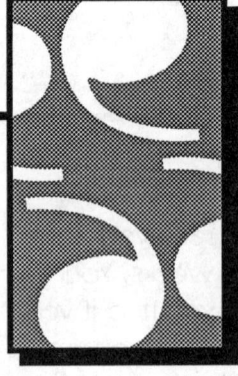

Evaluation

▶ Have you ever had an experience like the situation described in the role play? Describe it. What did you do?

_____
_____
_____
_____
_____

▶ Is it easier for you to brainstorm solutions to problems by yourself or with a group? Why?

_____
_____
_____
_____
_____

▶ What is one thing you could do to better resolve a problem you have now?

_____
_____
_____
_____
_____

Inside of Me

> **Objective:** Students will identify and create a list of things they like and do not like about themselves and from this list some set personal goals.

Materials ▶
- overhead projector
- worksheet on page 86
- evaluation on page 87

Journal Starters ▶
It is difficult for me to identify the things I like and don't like about myself because . . .
Some goals I set for myself are easy to reach because . . .
Some goals I set for myself are difficult to reach because . . .

Visualization ▶
Encourage students to think of a goal they have not yet reached. Invite them to close their eyes and think of a plan to attain it. Encourage students to visualize themselves reaching the goal. Invite students to describe the feeling of accomplishment they are visualizing.

Activity ▶
1. Make a transparency of the worksheet on page 86.
2. Give each student a copy of worksheet and encourage students to complete the worksheet as you guide them.
3. Share some of your own likes and dislikes as students complete the worksheet.
4. After the students have completed listing their likes and dislikes, demonstrate how to write goals from the list.

Likes or Dislikes	**Goals**
I don't like taking time to do things for other people.	⇒ I will clean out my closet and donate the things I don't need.
I like playing tennis.	⇒ I'll improve my game by playing three times a week.
I do not like getting bad grades.	⇒ I'll get a C in the two classes I'm failing.

5. Discuss with the students how setting goals can help them feel good about themselves. Invite students to share how they turned their dislikes into goals.
6. Invite each student to complete the evaluation on page 87.

Setting Goals - 85

Name _____ Date _____

Likes, Dislikes, and Goals

▶ One of the most important things in life is being honest with yourself. It's not always easy to recognize what you like or don't like about yourself. Some days it is easier to see the negative and forget about the positive. Take a really good look at yourself as you record what you like and don't like about who you are. Then, set five goals for yourself that will help you get better at the things you like or change some of the things you don't like.

▶ **Things I Like About Myself**

1. _____
2. _____
3. _____
4. _____
5. _____

▶ **Things I Don't Like About Myself**

1. _____
2. _____
3. _____
4. _____
5. _____

▶ **Goals**

1. _____
2. _____
3. _____
4. _____
5. _____

Name _____ Date _____

Inside of Me

Evaluation

▶ The one thing I like most about myself is _____
_____
_____

▶ The one thing I like least about myself is _____
_____
_____
_____

▶ The hardest thing about reaching my goals is _____
_____
_____
_____

▶ The last time I set a goal, I _____
_____
_____
_____

How Do I Feel About Myself?

Objective: Students will openly and honestly evaluate their qualities for the purpose of determining areas needing personal growth.

Materials ▶
- questionnaire on page 89
- evaluation on page 90
- *The Book of Qualities* by J. Ruth Gendler (optional)

Journal Starters ▶
I would define a quality as . . .
Some of the qualities I admire in a person are . . .
One quality I especially like about me is . . .

Visualization ▶
Encourage the students to think of someone they especially admire. Invite students to visualize how that person moves, speaks, reacts to situations, and treats other people.

Activity ▶
1. Create a transparency of the questionnaire.
2. Evaluate yourself while inviting students to listen as you think aloud and verbalize your thoughts. Modeling completing the questionnaire will encourage students to openly and honestly evaluate themselves. You may wish to read excerpts of quality personifications from *The Book of Qualities* by J. Ruth Gendler.
3. Give each student a questionnaire. Invite students to honestly evaluate themselves as you guide them through each question.
4. Encourage students to share some of their thoughts aloud as they complete the questionnaire.
5. Discuss with students how they can turn some of their qualities into goals. For instance, "I am helpful" can become the goal "I will begin doing the dishes after dinner at least two nights a week."
6. Encourage each student to complete the evaluation on page 90.

Name _____   Date _____

Personal Qualities Questionnaire

Evaluation

▶ Evaluate yourself by placing a check mark under the column "Never," "Seldom," "Often," or "Always" for each statement. Be honest and answer as accurately as possible.

▶ I am . . .	Never	Seldom	Often	Always
1. friendly	_____	_____	_____	_____
2. angry	_____	_____	_____	_____
3. happy	_____	_____	_____	_____
4. successful	_____	_____	_____	_____
5. sad	_____	_____	_____	_____
6. passive	_____	_____	_____	_____
7. brave	_____	_____	_____	_____
8. scared	_____	_____	_____	_____
9. loved	_____	_____	_____	_____
10. assertive	_____	_____	_____	_____
11. helpful	_____	_____	_____	_____
12. likable	_____	_____	_____	_____
13. trusted	_____	_____	_____	_____
14. truthful	_____	_____	_____	_____
15. cooperative	_____	_____	_____	_____
16. aggressive	_____	_____	_____	_____
17. thoughtful	_____	_____	_____	_____
18. considerate	_____	_____	_____	_____
19. loyal	_____	_____	_____	_____
20. healthy	_____	_____	_____	_____
21. jealous	_____	_____	_____	_____
22. shy	_____	_____	_____	_____
23. outgoing	_____	_____	_____	_____
24. confident	_____	_____	_____	_____

Name _____ Date _____

How Do I Feel About Myself?

Evaluation

▶ Which quality do you feel is your most positive? Why? _____
_____
_____

▶ Which quality do you feel needs the most growth? Why? _____
_____
_____
_____

▶ Write three goals based on qualities you checked with "Always."
_____
_____
_____
_____

▶ Write three goals based on qualities you checked with "Never."
_____
_____
_____
_____

I Can Do It

Objective:
Students will recognize that they have choices and can take charge of what happens to them by setting goals and thinking positively.

Materials ▶
- role play on page 92
- evaluation on page 93

Journal Starters ▶
In my life, I can choose to . . .
I have the power and control to change . . .
I feel . . . when I make decisions that . . .

Visualization ▶
Encourage students to visualize a time when they made a decision to change something in their lives, such as grades, a relationship, a way to make money, or a way to get something they wanted. Invite them to think about how they felt. Were they in control?

Activity ▶
1. Lead a discussion about times students were faced with a situation in which they procrastinated about making a decision or establishing a plan to reach their goal.
   - What were the circumstances?
   - Why did you avoid making a decision?
   - How did you feel? Why do you think you felt like that?
   - How would you deal with the situation if you were presented with it again?
2. Give each student a copy of the role play. Divide students into groups of three to rehearse. (You may wish to have students create their own role play instead.)
3. After an appropriate rehearsal time, invite each group to perform the role play.
4. Discuss students' feelings during the role play.
   - How did you feel when you knew you could succeed when others didn't feel you could?
   - Can you describe a time when you were in a similar situation? What happened? How did you feel?
   - If a friend were in a circumstance similar to Actor 1's, what would you do? Why?
5. Invite each student to complete the evaluation on page 93.

Setting Goals - 91

Name _____   Date _____

Attitude Is Everything

Role Play

Choose a role and rehearse it with your group members.

Actor 1

Try-outs are coming up for the city-wide tennis team. Trying out and making the team will require a lot of practice and time. You don't want your grades to suffer because of the time you spend playing tennis but you really want to give tennis a try. You wonder if you can play tennis and still remain on the honor roll. You discuss your options with Actors 2 and 3 while sitting in the cafeteria one day. You explain to your friends that with careful planning and a schedule of practice and study, you know that you can make the team and stay on the honor roll. You tell your friends that your parents have even relieved you of some of your household responsibilities so you can work towards your goal. You also tell Actors 2 and 3 that you have set aside some extra time with the tennis coach. You feel very confident that with hard work and determination, you can achieve your goal.

Actor 2

You listen very attentively to Actor 1 describe his or her goal of making the city-wide tennis team and remaining on the honor roll. You are supportive of the idea and offer ways you can help.

Actor 3

You listen to Actor 1 describe how he or she wants to make the tennis team while keeping good grades and then express that you do not think it is possible. You remind Actor 1 that the upcoming chemistry exam is impossible and that your English teacher is expecting a term paper due next week. You tell Actor 1 that there are many skilled tennis players who will also be competing to make the team and that Actor 1 doesn't stand a chance. You discourage Actor 1 from reaching his or her goal by saying that you know it can't be done.

92 - Setting Goals

Name _____ Date _____

I Can Do It

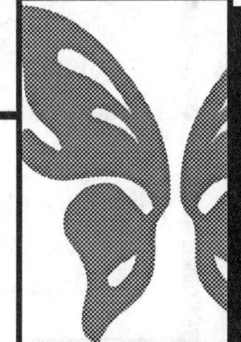

Evaluation

▶ How did Actor 2 feel about Actor 1's decision? _____
_____
_____

▶ Why do you think Actor 3 gave Actor 1 such a hard time? _____
_____
_____

▶ Would you give Actor 1 a hard time or try to support him or her? _____
_____
_____

▶ Have you ever been in a situation similar to Actor 1? What happened? How did you feel?
_____
_____
_____

▶ Do you think it's important to think positively when making decisions and choices? Why or why not?
_____
_____
_____

The Person I Admire

Objective: Students will reflect on people they admire to help them identify their own goals and dreams.

Materials ▶
- art paper
- colored pens or markers
- glue
- scissors
- magazines
- evaluation on page 95

Journal Starters ▶

When I think of someone I admire, I think that he/she is . . .
I wouldn't mind being like that person because . . .

Visualization ▶

Encourage students to think of a person they admire. What are this person's qualities and traits? In what ways would you like to be like this person? Why?

Activity ▶

1. Invite students to identify qualities they admire in a person.
2. Encourage students to think of a person they admire (celebrity, friend, teacher, family member) and make a collage depicting this person and his or her qualities.
3. After an appropriate amount of time, invite students to share their collages.
    - Why did you make this choice?
    - What are the qualities and successes that you admire about this person?
4. Encourage each student to complete the evaluation on page 95.

Name _____ Date _____

The Person I Admire

Evaluation

▶ One person I admire is _____
_____
_____

▶ I admire this person because _____
_____
_____
_____
_____
_____

▶ If I could have one quality of this person it would be _____

because _____
_____
_____
_____
_____

My Dream

> **Objective:** Students will identify their dreams and goals for the future and determine one thing they can do to reach their goals.

Materials ▶
- art paper
- colored pens or markers
- glue
- scissors
- magazines
- evaluation on page 96

Journal Starters ▶

The dream I have for my future is . . .

If a movie were being made about my life, I would like for it to include a part where I . . .

Visualization ▶

Invite students to close their eyes and visualize themselves living their dreams. What are the rewards? What are the obstacles they've overcome. How do they feel? Invite students to enjoy the feeling that they have reached their goals. What new goals do they have?

Activity ▶

1. Invite students to discuss their dreams and goals for the future. Discuss the importance in having goals, making steps to achieve the goals, and rewards.

2. Encourage students to create drawings or writings that depict their goals and dreams. Students may choose to draw their first initial very large and then fill it in with pictures that depict their dreams. Or, students may choose to create a treasure map showing the path to their goals. Along the way, pictures or symbols can depict the steps toward the ultimate goal. Another option might be to write a poem and illustrate it.

3. After an appropriate amount of time, invite students to share their creations.
   - What are your dreams and goals?
   - Do you think they are attainable?
   - How do you plan to reach your goals?
   - Why it is important to have dreams and goals?

4. Invite each student to complete the evaluation on page 96.

96 - Setting Goals

Name _____ Date _____

My Dream

Evaluation

▶ My goal for the future is _____
_____
_____

▶ I will achieve this goal by _____
_____
_____
_____
_____

▶ I think it is important to have goals because _____
_____
_____
_____
_____

Me... About Myself Re-Evaluation

Objective: Students will openly and honestly evaluate themselves for the purpose of determining how they have changed since the beginning of this program.

Materials ▶
- self-evaluation questionnaire on page 10

Final Activity ▶

This activity is an effective way to end the program outlined in this resource. It provides students with an opportunity to honestly assess who they have become and to measure how they have progressed towards developing healthy self-esteem.

1. Give each student the questionnaire on page 10 to complete again.
2. Give students the original copy of the questionnaire for them to compare.
3. Discuss with students how they changed and grew as a result of the program by comparing these responses to the responses they gave at the beginning of the program.

Name _____ Date _____

Vocabulary/Concept Review

▶ Match each word/concept with its proper definition.

____ 1. Assertive   a. Behavior or communication that is easily influenced by circumstances

____ 2. Fantasy   b. Mental imagery

____ 3. "Cop out"   c. Non-verbal communication using our faces and bodies

____ 4. Aggressive   d. A process you can use to make your thoughts more positive

____ 5. Reality   e. Trying to put the blame on someone else

____ 6. Fact   f. A statement that is true

____ 7. Self-concept   g. Behavior or communication that is clear, rational, and straight-forward

____ 8. Responsible   h. Behavior or communication that expresses anger and confusion

____ 9. Passive   i. The way that people view themselves

____ 10. Body language   j. Being able to accept the blame or credit for an action

____ 11. Visualization   k. The way things really are

____ 12. Self-talk   l. Thoughts that aren't real

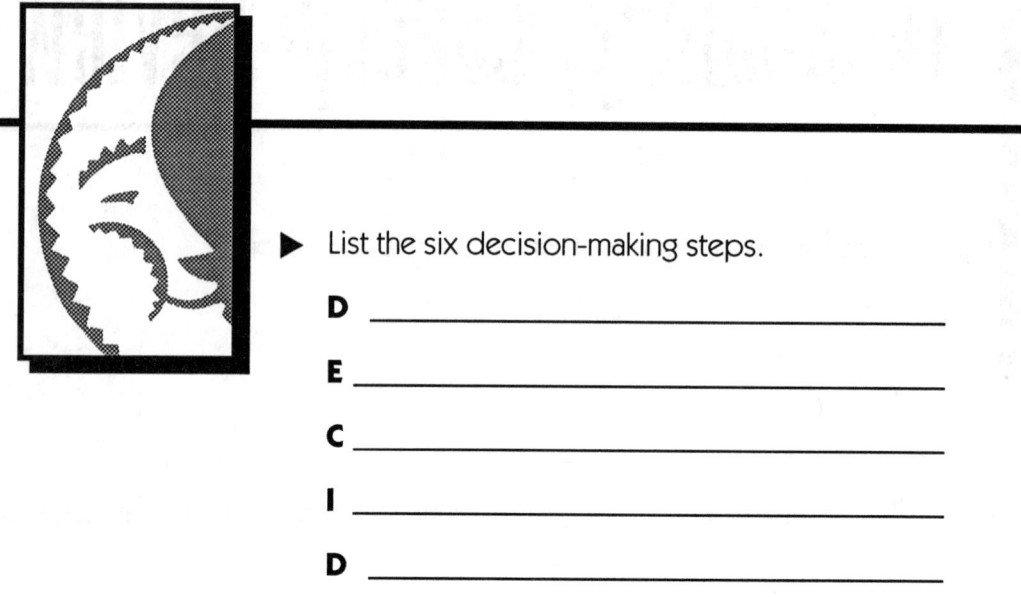

▶ List the six decision-making steps.

D _____
E _____
C _____
I _____
D _____
E _____

▶ List the six refusal steps.

R _____
E _____
F _____
U _____
S _____
E _____

▶ **Areas of Growth**
Compare your answers to the questionnaire you completed several weeks ago with your most recent answers to the questionnaire. Record areas in which you have changed or grown and explain what caused the growth.

_____
_____
_____
_____
_____

Vocabulary/Concept Review

Answer Key

▶ **Matching**
1. g
2. l
3. e
4. h
5. k
6. f
7. i
8. j
9. a
10. c
11. b
12. d

▶ **Six decision-making steps**
D etermine all possible choices presented by the situation.
E valuate and brainstorm all possible solutions.
C hoose a solution that makes sense to you.
I dentify with it! Visualize the outcome.
D evelop a plan and a schedule to follow.
E xamine the outcome of the plan and decision. Celebrate success!

▶ **Six refusal steps**
R eally ask questions about the activity.
E xamine all of the consequences.
F ind alternatives. Suggest different things to do.
U se persuasion. Be assertive.
S tate all of the consequences and problems.
E xit from the situation and leave doors open. No ultimatums.

▶ **Areas of Growth**
(Answers will vary.)

Behavioral Management

It is important that classrooms be places where teachers have opportunities to teach and students have positive learning environments. Safety and respect for both students and staff is extremely important and can be attained by using clear and concise school and classroom rules and consequences. A successful behavioral management program should include class meetings, clearly-defined class rules and consequences for breaking the rules, and most importantly, positive motivation.

Class Meetings ▶ Class meeting are an excellent way to address the behavior expected of your students and to establish class rules and consequences. In addition, this forum helps students understand democratic principles. Meetings should be held regularly and roles should be clearly-defined (chairperson, secretary, observer, timekeeper, and so on).

Class Rules and Consequences ▶ Class rules should be understood by students and displayed in a prominent place in the classroom. Some rules might include:
- Follow instructions without arguing.
- Respect others and their property.
- Work without disturbing others.
- Don't leave the classroom without permission.

Consequences for breaking rules should also be understood by students and displayed in a prominent place in the classroom. Consequences for breaking a rule might include the following progression:
- Warning
- Time out
- Note sent home
- Conference with parent

A behavioral contract is an effective way for students to be aware of and reflect upon inappropriate behavior. A sample behavioral contract is provided on page 104.

Behavioral Management

Positive Motivation ▶

To establish a healthy and creative learning environment, it is essential that you accentuate the positive. Negative behavior can be eliminated if students are motivated and rewarded for doing what is right. Establish a motivational system at the beginning of the year so students have a clear understanding of responsible and acceptable behavior. Some examples of positive and responsible behavior include:
- Working well without distracting others
- Respecting the rights of others
- Listening
- Being a good friend
- Being a good citizen
- Helping others
- Working well with others
- Caring about yourself

Present options from which students can choose as rewards for appropriate behavior. Awards may include:

Free Choice
Students can earn a five-minute "free choice" pass for great on-task behavior. What a student can do during "free choice" can be established at the beginning of the school year during a class meeting.

Raffle
Distribute raffle tickets to students at your discretion when students are acting responsibly. Hold weekly raffles for various prizes, such as soft drinks, pencils, "free choice" passes, or candy bars.

Coupons
Invite each student to create a coupon describing a reward he or she would like to receive. Create a contract for each student outlining what he or she needs to accomplish to redeem the coupon. You might want to encourage students to create additional uses for coupons as well.

Name _____ Date _____

Behavioral Contract

Evaluation

▶ I have been given a "time out" because I _____
_____
_____.

▶ The rule I broke was _____
_____
_____.

▶ The reason I broke the rule was because _____
_____
_____.

▶ Next time I am tempted to break this rule, I will _____
_____
_____.

▶ I am now ready to behave appropriately and follow classroom rules.

Student's signature _____

Teacher's signature _____

Journal Starters

▶ Here are some additional journal starters you might want to use as you continually motivate students to express their feelings in writing.

- My definitions of self-concept and self-esteem are . . .
- I think that . . . has a good self-concept because . . .
- One day that I really liked myself was when . . .
- The funniest thing I ever did was . . .
- One time I didn't like myself was when . . .
- I like it when people tell me that . . . because . . .
- Who am I today?
- My shadow can . . .
- List five things you are proud of and explain why.
- List ten words that describe you and explain why.
- Once when I told a lie . . .
- Once when I told the truth . . .
- Write down all the adjectives you can think of to describe someone you admire.
- List five things that are real and five things that are not.
- The worst dream I ever had was about . . .
- The best dream I ever had was about . . .
- Some "cop out" phrases I use are . . .
- I can change my "cop out" phrases to responsible statements by . . .
- My best friend is better at . . . This makes me feel . . .
- I think people are good at different things because . . .
- When I get angry I . . .

Journal Starters

- When someone is angry with me, I . . .
- When I am angry and upset, I should . . .
- I need . . .
- I want to tell . . . that . . .
- My feelings about myself are . . .
- When someone tells me about my behavior, I feel . . .
- Five facts are . . . Five beliefs are . . .
- This year I would like to . . . and I will do it by . . .
- In five years, I would like to . . . .
- I believe I can achieve my goals if I . . .
- Some goals that I have set for myself and reached include . . .
- Some goals that I have set for myself and haven't reached include . . .
- I find goals easier to reach if I . . .
- I think that I will be a success if I . . .
- The person I most admire is . . . I admire him/her because . . .
- I show I care about myself by . . .
- When I am feeling down I like to . . .
- When I have done something really well, I celebrate by . . .
- I know I have done something well when . . .
- The best thing I have ever done is . . .
- The worst thing I have ever done is . . .
- The most exciting thing that I have ever experienced is . . .
- The scariest thing that I have ever experienced is. . .

Visualizations

▶ It is often a good idea to create visualizations that address issues faced by several group members. You can expand on several of the ideas listed below or invite members of the group to create visualizations for various meetings. These ideas can be related to the topic that the group is working on or they can be related to journal starters. The more the group is involved in creating their own journal and visualization activities, the stronger the bonding within the group. Ideas generated by a group may be compiled into a special booklet for each group member to have.

▶ Use these questions as you encourage students to create mental images.
- What colors can you see?
- What sounds can you hear?
- What can you smell?
- What can you feel?
- What can you taste?
- Are you relaxing?
- Can you become a part of the experience?
- What emotions can you feel?
- Who was there?
- Who do you want to be there?
- What is happening?
- What do you want to happen?
- What do you want to do?
- Where do you want to do it?
- When do you want to do it?
- How would you do it differently?

▶ Use some of the following topics as you create visualizations.
- Winning a race
- Getting a good grade
- Winning a scholarship
- Making the team
- Reaching a goal
- Improving a relationship
- Seeing a high-spectrum, energizing color
- Being a quality
- Feeling an emotion
- Dealing with an emotion

Visualizations

- Going on an interview
- Getting a job
- Solving a problem
- Dealing with change
- Experiencing water, wind, or fire
- Creating a story
- Writing a poem
- Creating music
- Dealing with failure
- Being like someone you admire

▶ Below are some favorite, expanded visualizations.

Ocean
Listen to the sound of the ocean. You are the sea in all of its brilliant and varied shades of blue, green, and gray. You are clear and crisp and clean. The sunlight sparkles through you and you are constantly changing. You are the rhythm. You are the sound. You are the magic of the sea. Feel how united, powerful, gentle, and in control you are. Think of how wonderful you feel when you are poured and splashed. Since you are the sea, you know all the secrets, all the stories, and all the mysteries. You know the songs of the whales and the games of the dolphins. You are the music of the shore. The magical colors of the reefs depend on you. Without you, there would be no life on earth. Feel how important you are and how powerful you are in your ability to change. Listen to the sounds of the ocean. Become a part of it. The ocean is magic and so are you.

Wind
Can you hear the wind moving through the trees, rustling the leaves? Can you feel it on your skin and moving through your hair? Think about the wind moving over the world—able to move in an instant. Think about the wind entering gently through a window or powering a magnificent sailboat across the ocean. Become a part of the wind. You can generate electricity, bring rain, cool the air on a hot day, swirl falling snow, and travel swiftly over land. Think about a time when you really enjoyed the wind. Become the wind on that day. How do you feel? What are you doing? Can you feel your ability to work cooperatively with all other earth elements as you bring storms, clear away clouds, or change the seasons? You are important.

Visualizations

Crystal

Imagine a beautiful crystal. You are holding it in your hands. It has fire, rainbows, light, and brilliance inside of it. By moving it and holding it in different light, the colors within it come alive. It is ever changing, ever warm, and alive with its power to be constantly different. It can throw spectrums everywhere. This crystal is your very own. It will be easy to carry, always with you, and impossible to lose. You can look at it any time you want and use it whenever you need to center yourself. This crystal can be any kind, any size, any shape, and any color. Visualize your crystal. Feel the power, the creativity, the color. All of these things are inside of you and whenever you feel down or unsure of yourself, pull out your crystal and remember that you can use its qualities anytime you want.

Cave

Deep within all of us, there is a place inside where we go when things are difficult. Visualize this place as a beautiful crystal cave filled with diverse stalactites and stalagmites. They are the guardians of all of your fears, hopes, and dreams. In this place you can decide what is important and what you need to change. It is a place to safely go and decide if you are doing things in your life that will help you. It is the place where your most secret thoughts live and no one else can enter or take anything out of it. You can take things out of your cave and share them with others if you want to but you don't have to. Things that make you happy, angry, sad, proud, excited, or lonely can all stay in this cave safely. Visualize different caverns for different emotions. Remember, this is your thinking cave and that it can be anything you want. Listen to the quiet and watch the beautiful colors.

Visualizations

Treasure Map
Visualize a personal treasure map to help you reach your goals. Your goals may include passing a test or class, making a team, getting along better with others, losing weight, learning to play a musical instrument, saving money, or feeling better about yourself. Achieving your goals is like following a treasure map. Think of one particular goal and break it into small parts. Each small step is a point on your map. Create mental pictures to help keep you on task and visualize them along the way. If you take a wrong turn, don't give up. Think of a positive mental picture to get you back on track.

Flight
Listen to the music. Relax your body and concentrate on your thoughts and feelings. Let go of all your stress, anger, and confusion. Take flight. You are an eagle—strong and free, able to fly long distances and see everything below you. Fly out over the land and feel the wind holding you above the earth in its currents. Conserve your strength. Use it wisely and fairly and realize that the freedom of life lives within you. Feel the power. Know that power and strength are yours. You can always find this power and strength to help you through the roughest moments. When things get hard and you think that you can't make it through, become the eagle that lives within you. Take three deep breaths as you take flight. Fly up above everything and realize that by seeing the whole picture, you can find the strength and power you may need. Ride the currents and let yourself relax into your personal space of control and success.

Tree
There is a tree that lives inside of you. Your tree can help root you into the moment. Its branches can shelter and protect you. Visualize the roots reaching out of your feet into the earth's energy. Let them grow into the center of the earth. Let the energy of the earth travel up through the roots into you. Make it your own. Let the sheltering branches of the

Visualizations

tree reach up out of you. Let the branches surround, protect, shade, and shelter you. Let the wind gently blow through the leaves. Listen to the sound. Let it relax you. Let the branches reach towards the power of the sky. Let the energy surround you. Visualize energy in colors—green, white, bright pink. Think about what kind of tree you are. See it clearly and remember it.

Room
Whenever the things in your life are getting you down or seem too much to handle, visualize your own special room. In this room, place things that are really important to you—favorite books, games, activities, art, music, or "treasures." Make this room really comfortable and decorate it in a peaceful and creative way. Make it a room where you can make decisions and feel safe. This is your place. Perhaps you'd like a fireplace and a big comfortable chair. Perhaps you'll have a big picture window looking out over the mountains, sea, desert, or lake. Maybe you can see your tree out of the window. This will be a place for you to do your best work. Create this special place in your mind.

Bubble
Sometimes it is important to protect yourself when you are changing. The people who live around you sometimes don't know how to support your change or know how to help you. Sometimes your friends and family members will do things that make it easy to take a wrong turn. A brother or sister may offer you a piece of cake when you are on a diet. Your friends might try to talk you out of doing your homework. Realize that the changes you are trying to make and the goals you are trying to reach are sometimes scary to the people who care about you. You may need to place yourself in an imaginary bubble to focus on why you are trying to change. Visualize creating a bubble of beautiful translucent rainbow colors. Put yourself in this bubble and float up and above all the confusion and misunderstandings. Relax and visualize reaching your goals. Let that be the picture that keeps you on the path of your dreams. Keep bubbles around so you can play with them if you feel down. Listen and feel the peace and calm.

References

Anderson, Jill. *Thinking, Changing and Rearranging.*
Coopersmith, Stanley. *The Antecedents of Self-Concept.*
Dennis, Dr. Evie. *CATCH—Cognitive Affective Thinking Can Help.*
Gendler, Ruth. *The Book of Qualities.*
Goldstein, Arnold. *The Prepared Curriculum.*
Hancock, Ken and Barry Blaby. *People Interacting.*
Kranzler, Gerald and A. Ellis. *Pioneered Work in Rational Emotive Therapy and Cognitive Behavioural Training.*
Loescher, Elizabeth and Shirley Whiteside. *Conflict Management.*
Purkey, William W. *Self-Concept and School Achievement.*
Wragg, Jeffery. *Talk Sense to Yourself.*